LIVING AT TRACE

AMERICAN CHAPTERS

GRETA GORSUCH

WAYZGOOSE PRESS

CONTENTS

FROM THE AUTHOR

Welcome to our series, *American Chapters*. The *American Chapters* series presents short stories in vivid and easy-to-read 500-word chapters, perfect for English language learners internationally, and adult literacy learners in countries where English is commonly used.

All *American Chapters* print stories are also offered as audiobooks for learners who want to hear and read the stories and hear the sounds of American English.

American Chapters are lively, relevant, and realistic short stories about living in the United States of America. About Americans, immigrants, sojourners, and the diverse peoples living in this wide landscape, the stories touch on the tough questions, and the great things in life—things like work, ethnic differences, our connections to the past, our place in nature, being new, small town life, personal loss, and above all, new beginnings.

CHAPTER 1

"Who's this?" Brian asked. He sat under a large tree in front of his trailer. It was getting hot, now that it was June. He looked at the boy. The boy stood next to Ranger Jack Madison.

His hair was long and dark. His head was down. Brian couldn't see the boy's face.

Jack Madison said to the boy, "Mr. Longfield asked you a question." The boy said nothing. The two men waited.

Finally, Brian said, "What's your name? Come on. It's not a hard question." Brian and Ranger Jack Madison waited some more.

Finally, the boy said, "Tellman." He had a low voice. He was, Brian thought, about fourteen? Maybe fifteen? He was very thin. His clothes weren't clean. Didn't the boy's family take care of him?

"Nice to meet you, Tellman," Brian Longfield said. Another long wait.

The boy said, "Nice to meet you." After another minute, he said, "You can call me Tell."

Brian put his head to one side. He thought for a minute. Then, he looked at Ranger Jack Madison. Jack Madison brought the boy to the Lakeside Campground in his car. They all stood together under a large tree next to the lake.

Brian and Jack Madison worked at Trace State Park. It was a fishing and camping park in northern Mississippi. Jack Madison was a ranger at the park. A park ranger was sort of like being the police. His job was to drive around the park. He stopped and talked to campers. He gave directions. He made sure people weren't taking too many fish from the lake. He gave talks on the history of the park. He was also an expert on the animals in the park. If there was a bad storm, he made sure people at the park were safe. If there was bad trouble, his job was to take care of it. That was the "police" part of the job.

Brian's job at Trace State Park was different. Brian was a campground host. His job was to stay at the Lakeside Campground. He kept an eye on things. When someone new came to camp or fish, he greeted them. He took their money for the campsites. He told them where they could camp. He helped them use the water and electricity at each campsite. He told campers the rules. Sometimes people stayed up too late and played loud music. He would ask them to quiet down. He also helped campers if they had problems with their trailers. He was good at repairing things like televisions and toilets. He sometimes did repair work for the campers at the park. Last week, he found a small dog at the park, lost and alone. He spent several days calling campers who left to go home. He thought someone forgot the dog.

"Did you lose your dog?" he asked. No one said they lost their dog.

Brian then asked Jack Madison, "So, what's up?"

"Well, I have a small problem, here. And I think you may have an answer," Ranger Madison said.

"Oh?" Brian said. He was busy this morning. His sister-in-law, Darla, was going to arrive tomorrow. She was bringing her two kids, Willa and Dale. He had a lot to do to get ready.

"Yes. Just hear me out. See what you think," Ranger Madison said.

CHAPTER 2

"Tellman here got into trouble yesterday," Ranger Madison said. "He got picked up by the police. He stole some food from the supermarket."

"What?" Brian asked.

"Yeah," Jack Madison said. "Not the usual thing young people steal. Usually it's cell phones or video games. Not food."

The boy, Tell, seemed to get smaller. He kept his head down.

"What kind of food did he steal?" Brian asked.

"He stole some apples, some potato chips, and some dog food. He was eating an apple when they caught him," Ranger Madison said. "Someone from the supermarket saw him and called the police. They saw him two or three times, doing the same thing."

"Really? Dog food? What for?" Brian asked.

"Yeah," Jack Madison said. "Actually, the supermarket workers called the police because they were worried about him. Not because he was stealing food. Kids don't usually steal food."

"Right," Brian said. They were quiet for a minute. "Well, you should tell me what you want me to do."

"Right," Ranger Madison said. "Tellman says he was living out here at Trace last week. I want to know if you remember him."

"What? I don't think so," Brian said. Brian turned to look at Tell. "Tell, do you mean you were living here, at Lakeside Campground?"

"Yes," Tellman said, "But it was that campground. Back there in the trees." He pointed behind the men, to the right, toward the end of the park.

That campground was called Opa Campground. "Opa" was the Chickasaw word for "owl." Trace State Park was once Chickasaw land, and the Chickasaw Indians lived there for hundreds of years. Opa Campground was the far end of the park. There were deep, dark trees. Even in the bright hot sun, that part of the campground looked dark. It was quiet, but there were lots of mosquitoes. Not many campers wanted to stay back there. There was no water or electricity. It was far from the shower building. Sometimes, at night, you could hear an owl. "Whoooo... whooo whoo whoo WHOOO...," it said, up in the dark trees.

"OK," Brian said. "So, you were back there in Opa Campground. Can you tell me the dates you were here? Who were you with? What name should I look under?"

Tell answered, "I don't know the dates. We were living on the road for two or three months. I lost track of time. My dad took us out of school."

Both Jack Madison and Brian were surprised. They were quiet for a minute. *Us?* thought Brian. *Living on the road for two or three months? What kind of family is this?*

Tell looked so sad that Brian wanted to ask questions again. He hated that a young boy like this looked so sad. Fourteen or fifteen was too young to feel such sadness. If Brian kept talking, and could find some answers, maybe Tell wouldn't feel so sad. Or, maybe Brian wouldn't have to see this young boy's sadness.

"Yeah," Ranger Jack Madison said. "Go on."

"My dad, my little brother Rio, and dad's girlfriend... and... Handy, my dog," Tell said. "We were here four days ago. I think."

CHAPTER 3

"OK," Brian Longfield said. "Can you tell me your dad's name?"

"It's Sykes. Dave Sykes," Tell said.

"Does that mean your name is Tellman Sykes?" Ranger Jack Madison asked. He wrote Tell's name down.

"Yes… yes. My name is Tellman Sykes. And my little brother's name is Rio," Tellman said. "He's seven years old."

"You think you were here four nights ago?" Brian asked.

"Yes," the boy's voice was quiet. "Look I'm really sad about my dog, Handy. I think he's out here at the park. He might be hungry. That's why I got the dog food. I wanted to walk out here. I wanted to find him."

"I think your dog is fine," Brian said. "I have him. Is he small, gray, with short hair? Likes to eat?"

"Yes!" Tell said.

"Can you tell me anything else about him?" Brian asked.

"He has a long tail. And he likes to sleep on the bed," Tellman said. "He's not very old. Do you have him? Can I see him?"

"Of course," Brian said. "I'll get him from my trailer." He said to Ranger Madison, "I'll get my campground notebook. If Tell's family was here, I can find their information. Maybe."

Brian went into his trailer and found the little dog. He was a small dog, but Brian thought he was a good friend, too. He was friendly. He liked to play. And yes, he liked to sleep on the bed with Brian. He asked the dog to come outside. He said "Handy! Come here!" and the dog barked and turned around and around and around. "Yeah," thought Brian, "that's Tell's dog." Brian got his campground notebook. Then he went outside to the tree where Tell and Ranger Madison were waiting.

Handy the dog ran to Tellman as fast as he could. Tell and Handy looked happy together. Brian looked away. It was a happy sight. But it was also hard for him to see it. Since his wife Nancy died in March, just four months ago, Brian had these strange, still moments. He didn't know if he was sad, or happy. He missed Nancy. But he also thought everything looked more beautiful because he missed her. He thought sometimes he could see her in the blue, cool water of the lake. There was a lot of beauty in Trace State Park. As the weather got warmer, the trees got greener. The lake became darker, and more blue.

CHAPTER 4

Ranger Jack Madison and Brian Longfield watched Tell play with Handy, the little gray dog. There was no question Handy was Tell's dog. While Tell sat down under the tree by the lake, he held Handy. It was the first time Brian saw Tell smile.

Brian looked at his campground notebook and told Ranger Jack Madison, "I see here four nights ago that a family named "Smith" stayed at Opa Campground, site number 4. It's back there in the trees."

"OK," Ranger Madison said. "They probably didn't give their real name."

"Right," Brian said. "I remember the father now. Big, with dark hair. I didn't like him. He kept looking around. He wouldn't look me in the eye. He had an old car, green in color. I guess they slept in a tent. I heard him shouting back there in the trees once. I was going to talk to him the next day but everyone was gone. I never saw Tell. I never saw any kids. I did see the girlfriend. Pretty, blonde hair. But she was asleep in the car."

"So, Sykes lied about his name. He used the name Smith?" Ranger Madison asked.

"Yes, I think so. But I got his car license number. That doesn't lie. Here it is," Brian said. "Alabama 766-163."

"Good. That's a start," Ranger Madison said. "Tellman is staying with me and my family for a few days. I know the police in Pontotoc. They called me about him. There's no other good place for Tellman to go right now."

"OK. But....I think I should keep Handy for now," Brian said. "When the state of Mississippi decides to take care of Tell, then we can decide what to do with his dog."

"Good thing," Ranger Madison said.

He and Brian watched Tell and Handy for a few minutes. Then he talked to Tell about Brian's plan. Brian would keep Handy for a few days. Tell wasn't happy about leaving his dog behind. But he said, "Thanks for taking care of my dog."

He and Ranger Madison got into the park ranger's car. They drove along the lake to Opa Campground. Ranger Madison wanted to look for anything from the Sykes family. Maybe some papers or maps? A backpack? Anything that might tell him where the Sykes family was now. But he didn't find anything but mosquitos and dark trees.

CHAPTER 5

Brian woke up the next morning. The sun was just coming up. He went outside his trailer to drink a cup of hot tea. Even though it was hot in Mississippi in June, he still enjoyed his tea hot. He called to Handy the dog, who was still asleep. After Handy saw Tell yesterday, it was hard to get Handy to sleep. He was so happy to see Tell again. Finally, around two in the morning little Handy settled down and went to sleep.

Handy came outside and walked around the trees and grasses. Brian watched him in the morning sunlight. He thought about what happened the day before. He thought about Tell, that sad thin boy. He thought about Tell's little brother, Rio. He wondered where Rio was right now. It was not good for a seven-year-old boy to be without his big brother. He thought about Tell's father, who called himself "Smith." Brian did not like the man. He looked like he would shout, or say bad things. He looked like he would do bad things. Tell's father lied about his name. And then he left Tell, and Handy. He left Tell in Pontotoc, far from home in Alabama. He took Tell and Rio out of school. And he left Handy at Trace State Park. Anything could happen to a small dog like that. This is not what a good man, or a good father, would do.

Brian finished his tea. He had a lot to do today. His sister-in-law Darla, and her two children were coming today. Darla telephoned last night and said they would be there around lunchtime.

Brian walked to each campsite at the Lakeside Campground. It was his job. It was Tuesday, so the Lakeside Campground was only half full. That meant there were about 15 campsites with people in them. They were mostly family groups. There was a mother and a dad, with two or three children. Most families were from Mississippi, but a few were from Alabama or Tennessee. These states were nearby. Camping in the summer was something young families did. It didn't cost much money. On Friday, Trace State Park would be full of people. Most campers liked to go camping on weekends. Friday and Saturday nights were the most busy. People enjoyed the lake, and the beauty of the park. The air was always fresh. If campers wanted to go into town to buy food,

Pontotoc was only 15 minutes away. It was a nice town. People were friendly. There were lots of shops and businesses. Brian went to Pontotoc once a week.

Brian enjoyed walking around the Lakeside Campground with Handy. He was a good dog. He seemed to understand people. He watched them. If he thought a person was friendly, he went over to see them. If he didn't think a person was friendly, he stayed near Brian. If Tellman found a home, he would take Handy with him. That was good. But Brian would miss Handy. A lot.

CHAPTER 6

Brian walked back to his trailer with Handy at his side. He saw a blue car drive up. It was his sister-in-law Darla, and her children, Willa and Dale. He went to the car, and the car doors opened.

Dale, his nephew, called out "Uncle Brian! We're here!"

Then he saw Handy, the small gray dog. "Uncle Brian, did you get a DOG?" And Handy went to Dale. He loved young boys. Dale was seven. Dale loved dogs. Darla got out of the car and hugged Brian. "Oh, it's good to see you," she said.

"Right back at you," Brian said. He called out to Willa, who stayed in the car. "Hey Willa! Come on out!"

After a minute, Willa, a 15-year-old girl, got out of the car. She looked at Brian. Then, without a word, she turned away. She walked to the lake.

"Oh boy," Brian said. "She really is a pain."

Darla said, "Yes. She's a pain even on good days. But this week, maybe she has a reason why." Darla looked at Brian. She said, "Look, Willa is angry with me."

"Why?" Brian asked.

"Brian," Darla said, "my husband left me." Brian just looked at her.

"Brian," Darla said again, "my husband left me." Darla looked so sad. She wore a green skirt. She had long, curly brown and gray hair. She was a pretty woman. She took care of herself. But her face was sad, and her shoulders were bent over. She stood there by the car. She couldn't seem to move.

Brian didn't say anything for a minute. He thought of what to say. What do you say to a dear friend who is so unhappy? Well, the news was no big surprise to Brian. Darla's husband left her. Brian only met him once. His name was Rick. Rick may have said, "Hello," and that was all, before he turned on the TV. He was a truck driver. He was always gone. It wasn't fair to Darla, who was a good wife. She was with her kids, Dale and Willa, by herself, most of the time.

Brian said, "I'm sorry, Darla. I'm so sorry. When did that happen?"

"The day before we left," Darla said. "Rick was gone,

driving his truck to Alabama, or somewhere. I can't remember. Then he called me. He told me he met someone else. He wasn't coming back home." Darla stopped talking. She started to cry a little.

Brian went to her. He took her to the chairs he kept under the tree. They sat down. Dale and Handy, the little dog, followed. They played together in the shade under the tree. Even though Dale played with the dog, Brian thought that Dale was listening to what his mother said.

After a few minutes, after Darla stopped crying, Brian asked her, "What do you plan to do?"

Darla answered, "I was thinking we could stay here for a few weeks. I got us a room at that motel. You remember the one outside the park? It's just a few minutes away. Willa and Dale aren't in school. It's summer now."

Brian said, "That's a good idea. I like it. I can get to know Dale and Willa better." Then he asked, "But what are you going to do all day?"

CHAPTER 7

Brian Longfield, and Darla, his sister-in-law, talked about her visit to Mississippi. Brian was happy he could spend time with Dale and Willa. He asked Darla, "But what are you going to do all day?"

Darla said, "I might look for a job. Just for a few weeks. I have a few telephone numbers to call. Businesses are always looking for someone who's good in an office. I know how to use computers. I sound nice. I'm good on the telephone."

When they arrived at Lakeside Campground, Willa, Darla's 15-year-old daughter, walked away. As usual, she didn't say anything. She looked angry. But as Darla talked about her plans, Willa came back from the lake. She sat down under the tree next to Dale and Handy. By this time, Handy was worn out from all the playing and the sunshine. He was laying across Dale's legs, fast asleep. Willa reached over and touched Handy's soft head. Handy stretched and yawned. And then he fell asleep again. A few clouds came over the sun. Then the sun came out again. The shade from the clouds came and went. After some more time went by, Brian got everyone into his truck and they went to Pontotoc for lunch.

Pontotoc was a small town, so everyone knew everyone else. It was a friendly place, with shops, a post office, two banks, a book store, and lots of places to eat good southern food. It was an old town, dating from 1837. But the Chickasaw Indians lived there many years before that. Brian once looked at a street map for Pontotoc. He was surprised at how many streets names were from American Indian languages. There were streets names like "Choctaw Ridge," and "Coonewah Road." The town's name "Pontotoc" was a Chickasaw word for "Land of Hanging Grapes." Hundreds of years ago, there must have been grapes somewhere.

Brian took Darla and her children to a restaurant he liked called "Fishman's." It was an old-style place with great food. Brian ordered fried chicken, fried green tomatoes, and iced tea for everyone. Dale happily ate the food. He left nothing on his plate. Willa ate a little chicken but she wouldn't touch the fried green tomatoes. "Eewwwww," was all she said. "Is that what they eat here?"

"Shhhh," Darla said. "This is southern food. This is what they like to eat. Try some! It's good. Crispy but soft at the same time."

Willa didn't answer. She looked around at the tables filled with people. They were all eating, talking, and laughing. But Willa didn't see anything interesting. Bored, she looked at Brian and asked, "Uncle Brian?"

"Yeah?" Brian said, surprised. His mouth was full of crispy fried chicken.

"Where did you get that little dog?" Willa asked. Her little brother Dale looked interested. He loved dogs.

Brian answered, "Well, Handy was left here by a family last week. I found him in the woods, alone. He was small, afraid, and alone....and hungry. So, I took him in. I telephoned everyone who stayed at Opa Campground last week. No one said the dog was theirs."

"So, are you going to keep him?" Willa asked.

"I don't think so," Brian said. "Handy belongs to a boy named Tellman Sykes."

"Tellman?" Willa said, her voice rising high up. "What kind of name is Tellman?"

"Shhhh!" Darla said. "Tellman is a nice name. It's not strange or anything."

Brian smiled. He said, "He said to call him 'Tell'. He might be coming to visit Handy soon. You can meet him."

CHAPTER 8

After lunch, Brian and Darla bought a few things at a store. They bought some drinks, bread, cheese, fruit, tea, and coffee. Then they got back to the Southland Motel. It was five minutes away from the entrance of Trace State Park. The motel room where Darla, Willa, and Dale were staying had a small kitchen. It had a sink with water, and a refrigerator to keep things cold. Brian made sure Darla had a map of Pontotoc and Tupelo, a nearby city. She needed the map to find her way around.

"Mom?" Dale said, "Why don't you use a GPS? It's easier than a map."

Darla laughed. "Dale, we don't have money for a GPS. Besides I'm old fashioned. I like to look at maps. That way I can understand what a town is like." Brian smiled at that. That was how he was, too.

Brian knew the owner of the Southland Motel. His name was Jim. He was an older man, like Brian. Sometimes Brian repaired things at the motel. Sometimes a broken window, or a refrigerator. So, Jim was happy to give Darla and her children a larger room. The room had large windows, and a table and a desk. There was a place to sit and talk, and two large beds. The Southland Motel was old, but very clean. It was quiet, too. It was close enough to Trace State Park that Willa and Dale could visit Brian easily. If they walked to Brian's trailer in the park, it took twenty minutes. It was only 10 minutes to the ranger's station at the park entrance.

The motel was out in the country, but Brian found a junior high school nearby. He called the school, and found out their library was open all summer. Any child in the area could visit the library to read books. So, even though Dale was only seven, and Willa was fifteen, and already in high school, they could still use the library.

Brian told Willa and Dale to walk to the ranger's station at the park entrance at nine the next morning. He would pick them up in his truck and show them around Trace State Park. He would make lunch for them in his trailer.

"OK," Willa said, sounding bored.

"Willa!" her mother Darla said. "What's wrong with you?" Willa walked into the motel room and turned on the TV.

"OK, Uncle Brian," Dale said. He thought for a minute. "Could you show us Chickasaw Point?"

Brian laughed, "What? Where did you hear about Chickasaw Point?"

Dale said, "Mom told us about it. It's a campground at Trace State Park, right? You saw some lights out there at night? Mom said there was an Indian village there."

"True. Well, it's just a campground now, with families. You can't see where the Indian village was," Brian said.

"That's OK," Dale said, "I still want to see it."

CHAPTER 9

The next morning, Dale and Willa were waiting for Brian at the ranger's station. They were inside, talking to Ranger Jack Madison, and Maggie Morningstar, the park office manager. Maggie had light brown hair, and a warm smile. "Why Mr. Longfield, I had no idea you had a niece and nephew!" Willa was smiling. She liked Maggie Morningstar.

Ranger Madison said, "Dale has hardly stopped talking since they got here. He really wants to know about the park."

Brian laughed, "Yes, Dale likes to ask questions. But he listens, too."

Maggie Morningstar said, "Mr. Longfield, I can't remember the last time I heard you laugh. It's so great to hear you laugh."

Brian didn't know what to say. Nancy, his wife, died last March. It was only a few month ago. It didn't seem like there was anything to feel happy about. For a minute, everyone was quiet.

"Well," Brian said, "thanks for saying that."

Maggie Morningstar said, "I'm sorry, I didn't mean to...."

Brian answered, "Don't worry about it. Nancy is gone. It's just hard to get used to."

Ranger Madison made a noise like "AHEM!" and everyone jumped. "Right," Jack Madison said. He looked at Brian and said, "Brian, can I talk to you a few minutes?"

Brian said, "Sure." He told Dale and Willa to wait. Willa began talking to Maggie, while Dale looked around the ranger's station. There was a small library and museum there, all about Trace State Park.

Jack Madison said, "I wanted you to know that I have some information about Tellman Sykes' family."

Brian was interested. He said, "Yeah?"

Ranger Madison went on, "Yeah. I got a call from the police in Texas. They think Dave Sykes robbed two convenience stores in Lufkin. That's a small town in east Texas."

"WHAT?"

Brian was shocked.

"Yep. They had a camera in both stores. They got a call from the police in Alabama. Dave Sykes is in trouble there, too. The Alabama State Police saw the photos from the stores' cameras in Texas and said that was Dave Sykes."

"Wow," Brian said. He thought for a moment. Then he said, "So he robbed convenience stores in Alabama? Then he brought his family here to Mississippi. He dumped Tellman. And Handy, Tell's dog. Then he drove with his girlfriend, and Tell's little brother Rio, to Texas? And robbed more stores in Texas?"

"Yeah, you have it."

Brian had a bad feeling about it. Tell's little brother Rio was just seven years old. A young boy shouldn't be around someone who robbed stores.

Ranger Madison went on, "They think the girlfriend is the driver, for when Dave Sykes robs a convenience store. He does the robbing. He has a gun. Then he runs out to the car. And then she drives away."

"Oh, no." Brian could think of nothing more to say.

CHAPTER 10

Brian Longfield and Jack Madison were talking in the ranger's station at Trace State Park. It was a bright, sunny morning. It was going to be very, very warm out. Well, it was June in Mississippi. Mississippi was a southern state in the U.S., and they had very hot summers.

Ranger Jack Madison finished talking about Tellman Sykes' father, Dave Sykes. The man, and his girlfriend, were convenience store robbers. And now Tellman's little brother, Rio, was in a bad spot. A seven-year-old boy should not be in a car, on the road somewhere, with two robbers who had a gun.

"Where is Tellman's mother?" Brian asked.

"No one knows," Jack Madison said. "The police in Alabama are looking for her."

Then Brian said, "How is Tellman, anyway? Is he eating more? I never saw such a thin, sad young boy like that."

Ranger Madison laughed, "Oh yes, he's eating. My wife can't keep up with him. You know we have three young children at home. Having a 15-year-old in the house takes a lot of work. Tell's a good kid. But he's worried about his little brother Rio. And, he got dumped here in Mississippi without food or any help. Even though his father Dave Sykes is no good, I'm sure Tellman feels sad about being left behind that way."

"Oh yeah," Brian said. He thought for a minute and said, "I have my niece and nephew here. Willa is the same age as Tell. And Dale is the same age as Rio. While their mom's at work, I'm keeping them with me. We'll work at the park together, or I'll take them to the library at the junior high school. You should bring Tell to Trace State Park tomorrow. He can stay with us. He might like talking to Dale since he's so worried about his little brother. Dale is a smart, quick little boy. Maybe he will remind Tell that Rio is a smart, quick little kid, too. Rio might be OK."

Ranger Jack Madison said, "You know, that's a great idea! Are you sure it's OK?"

"I think it's fine," Brian said. "I'll tell the kids. I pick them up at nine in the morning, right here at the ranger's station. You can bring Tell with you."

"Great!" Jack Madison said.

Brian went out to tell Willa and Dale his plan. Maybe Willa was happy because she was talking to Maggie Morningstar. She was interested in meeting Tell. Well, at least she didn't walk away and look angry. Dale, on the other hand, was excited to meet him. He asked lots of questions. "Why's his name Tellman? Where's he from? Does he like to read? Does he want to go to the library with us? Does he like going to Indian villages? Can we have lunch with him? What does he like to eat? Does he have brothers and sisters?" And on and on.

Brian answered as many questions as he could. He did not tell Willa and Dale about Tellman's family. He did not say how Tell was left alone. That Tell was stealing food from a supermarket so he could eat. Finally, Brian laughed and said, "I can't keep up with your questions!" Everyone laughed as Brian, Willa, and Dale got in the truck to see the park. He drove them to Chickasaw Point Campground. This was a beautiful campground with tall trees. You could walk by the lake and enjoy the cool looking water. The wind was strong there, so there weren't many mosquitoes. In the summer, there were many families camping there. When Brian first saw Chickasaw Point, it was winter. The campground was closed then. But today, it was full of life. Children ran and played, and their mothers and fathers sat under the tall trees.

Brian showed Dale where the Indian village was, hundreds of years ago. It was right by the water. They both stood and enjoyed the wind, the water, and the trees.

CHAPTER 11

It was a good day. Brian showed Willa and Dale the other campgrounds in the park. He showed them Opa Campground, back in the deep woods. The kids enjoyed it, but there were too many mosquitoes. They left after just a few minutes.

"When it gets colder, the mosquitoes go away," Brian said.

"Then the campground has owls, and lot of other birds and animals."

They went to Brian's trailer and had lunch. Willa took a few bites of the cheese sandwich Brian made for her and then pushed it away. Handy, the little gray dog, looked at the sandwich. He wanted some.

"She wishes she had fried green tomatoes now!" Dale said, laughing.

Willa laughed, which surprised Brian. She asked, "Do you have any vegetables?" Brian took some salad and some grapes out of the refrigerator and Willa ate every bit. Brian gave Handy a very small piece of cheese from Willa's sandwich. After lunch, Brian took the kids on a tour of Lakeside Campground.

He showed them the different campsites. There were thirty in all. About half of them had campers. Some young families were there. They were staying in tents. Brian said hello to people at each campsite. He asked if everything was OK. One young couple said they were having trouble with the water at their campsite. The husband and wife were good friends of Brian's. They came to Lakeside Campground last February. They brought their three young children with them from Indiana. There were no jobs in Indiana, and both the husband and wife found jobs quickly in Tupelo nearby. They were saving money to buy a house. The wife was very good to Brian after Nancy died. She brought food when Brian was too sad to cook, or to eat well. She visited every morning, and drank coffee with Brian before she left for work.

Brian was happy to help them. Their trailer was old, and it needed a lot of repairs. As Brian looked at their trailer, Willa came to help. Brian was very surprised to learn that Willa was good at repairing things. She enjoyed it. She was only 15, and she didn't know much yet. But she had a good feel for doing repairs, and she helped Brian. Brian told Willa what he was doing, step by step. She asked questions and he answered them. Quickly, the repair was done. The trailer had water so the young wife could wash dishes inside.

Brian, Dale, and Willa said good-bye, and walked along the lake to the end of Lakeside Campground. It was hot, but there was some wind. This meant it was cooler, and there were fewer mosquitoes.

Darla, their mother, came to pick up her kids at 3 PM. Darla told Brian about her new job. It was in Tupelo at a flower shop. She enjoyed it. It didn't pay much, but it was her first job in Mississippi. She might find something better, if they stayed.

While Willa and Dale waited in the car for their mother, Brian told Darla about Tellman Sykes. He told her about how Tell came to Mississippi, and about Tell's little brother Rio.

"Oh, I think he should spend time with Willa and Dale," Darla said. "They're a little lonely, and he is, too. But are you sure it's safe?"

"What? Why?" Brian asked.

"Well, that father of Tell's might show up again. If he's robbing convenience stores and has a gun...well, that's not good," Darla said.

"I thought of that," Brian said, slowly. "But all three kids will be with me. I won't let anything happen. And the police are looking for Dave Sykes and that girlfriend of his. The police might catch them."

That night, as Brian fell asleep in his trailer, he heard two owls calling in the distance. That was strange. Usually owls called in the winter, but now it was June.

CHAPTER 12

The next morning, Ranger Jack Madison was there with Tellman Sykes.

"Tell looks better," Brian thought. "He's not so thin. And he isn't looking down all the time." Tell still had long hair, but it was clean. He saw Brian and waved his hand. "Hi Mr. Long-field," he said.

Brian, Willa, Dale, and Handy, the dog, got out of the truck. Handy ran to Tell as fast as his little legs would go. As Tell petted Handy, Willa and Dale came up. Dale was soon asking lots of questions, what did Tell like to eat? Did he like to read? Did he know there was an old Indian village at Chickasaw Point Campground? Did he live in a trailer? Where was he from? Tell was still quiet and shy, but he did his best to answer Dale's questions. Willa wanted to know how Tell got his name.

"Tellman?" she asked. "What kind of name is that?" She was smiling when she asked.

"Um...," Tell said, looking down. "That's my grandfather's name."

"Oh, OK," she said.

Brian said to Ranger Madison, "I'll bring Tell back here around four. Is that okay?"

Jack Madison said it was OK. Then he said quietly, "Brian, the police have found Tell's mother."

"That's very good news," Brian said. "Is she coming here?"

"Yes. From what the police said, it seems Dave Sykes took both Tellman and Rio away. He never told her where he was going. He just took those two boys and never went back. She's been crazy with worry for over three months," Ranger Madison said. He looked angry. How could any father do that to his own kids? "Anyway," he said, "she should be here in two or three days. Maybe Saturday sometime?"

"Does Tell know?" Brian asked.

"Yeah, I told him this morning. That's why he looks so happy," Ranger Jack Madison said.

Brian got into his truck with three kids and Handy the dog.

It was a tight fit, but everyone laughed as the truck rolled down the road. They went to the junior high school library and looked for books. They spent two happy hours reading and talking quietly. Dale found two books on the Chickasaw Indians. He wanted to learn more about them. He found the word "opa" in one book and told Brian it meant "owl." "So," Dale said, "Opa Campground means Owl Campground!"

"Right," Brian said.

Then Dale said, "Well, this book also says that owls were very important to the Chickasaw Indians."

"Oh?" Brian said, interested.

"Yeah! It says that owls brought messages to people. AND sometimes if an owl called near your home, someone might die," Dale said.

"Oops," Brian said. "I heard two owls last night over at Opa Campground."

"Oh," Dale said.

"It's a little strange to hear them in summer. Maybe we're getting some storms soon, or something. But owls are nothing to be afraid of. They just fly and hunt. Have you seen an owl? They're beautiful," Brian said. He went over to the library computer and found a website on owls.

"Here it is," he said. "This is the kind of owl I heard." He pushed a computer key and an owl call played. "Whoooo... whooo whoo whoo WHOOO!" Brian showed Dale a picture of the owl. It was small, and brown and white, with large golden eyes.

"Oh," Dale said.

CHAPTER 13

The next day, everyone went fishing at the lake. Of the four camp-grounds at Trace State Park, Chickasaw Point had the best fish-ing. Brian took Willa, Dale, and Tell to a good spot at Chickasaw

Point, under some tall trees. They had chairs and fishing poles. Pretty soon, Tell caught a fish, and so did Brian. The fish were small, so they threw them back into the cool, blue lake. It was a hot day. But Brian saw some dark clouds to the west. That meant a storm tonight, with rain and wind. But for now, if everyone stayed in their chairs and didn't move, they could stay cool. After a few hours, they gave up and returned to Lakeside Campground.

They made lunch, and Maggie Morningstar came over from the ranger's station. She brought fried green tomatoes, and Brian made hamburgers. Willa ate three of the fried green tomatoes. Dale laughed the whole time. "I thought you didn't like southern food?" he said.

Willa just smiled back and took another fried green tomato. "I changed my mind," she said. Then she turned to Tell. She asked, "Do you like southern food?"

Tell said, "Well, I'm from Alabama. That's in the south, I guess. I like our food."

Willa asked, "What kinds of food do you eat? What does your mom like to make?"

"Uh," Tell said. "Uh, my mom likes to make sweet potatoes. And fried fish. And she's good at peach pie."

"What's your mom's name?" Dale asked.

"She's Melinda, Melinda Sykes," answered Tell.

"She'll be here in just a few days," Brian said.

But Willa was not done with her questions. "What's school like in Alabama?" Willa asked.

"It's OK, I guess. I haven't been in school since March. I kind of miss it," Tellman said.

There were five seconds of complete silence.

"What?" Willa said, finally. "How can you miss three months of school?"

Tell looked at Brian. Brian said, "If you want to tell her, you can. But if you don't want to, then don't."

But Tell finally answered, "My father took me and my little brother out of school. He took us away from our mother. He put us in a car. Then he picked up his girlfriend. And then we left town. We never went back."

Little Dale went to where Tell was sitting, and put his hand on Tell's arm. "What's your brother's name?" Dale asked.

"Rio," Tell said, in a very small voice. "When dad left me and Handy behind, he took Rio with him. I don't know where Rio is now."

Finally, Maggie Morningstar spoke. She said, "Tell, I'm really sorry to hear that. But the police will find Rio, I know it. Brian found Handy here, and now you have your little dog back. You'll get Rio, too."

That night, after everyone left to go home, a storm came to Trace State Park. The dark clouds in the west became black. Finally, the entire sky was dark, and filled with rain and wind. It rained until 2 AM, and Brian woke up. Again, he heard the two owls calling in the dark forest. "Whoooo...whooo whoo whoo WHOOO!" one said, far away. "Whoooo...whooo whoo whoo WHOOO!" the other said, much closer, over in Opa Campground. Brian thought about the Chickasaw Indian story. If an owl calls at night, it means someone might die.

CHAPTER 14

It was Saturday morning. Today, Melinda Sykes would come. Tell could hardly keep quiet. It was the most Brian ever heard him talk. He kept asking, "When's mom coming?" and "Do you think the storm stopped her from driving here?" It was true that last night's storm was pretty bad. It moved from

west to east, into Alabama. Alabama was where Melinda Sykes
was driving from. Brian and Tell were waiting for Willa and
Dale at the ranger's station at the entrance to Trace State Park.
Ranger Jack Madison got a phone call and left suddenly to
drive to Pontotoc. He didn't say where he was going.

The morning was very quiet. Most of the campers left the
day before. They didn't want to camp out in the storm. Maggie
Morningstar didn't have anything to do. So, she told Tell,
"Come over here. I'll cut your hair. You can't look like that
when your mother comes."

So, Maggie and Tell went outside under a tree. Maggie cut
Tell's dark hair. He looked like a different boy when Maggie
was done. You could see his face for the first time. He was a
good-looking boy. He was still thin, but he was excited and
happy now. His mother was coming.

Brian got a call on his cell phone. It was Darla. "Brian!"
she said. "Turn on the TV! There's a story about a robbery in
Pontotoc!"

Maggie came in with Tell. Brian asked her if there was a TV
he could watch. "We don't have a TV here," she said. "But we
do have a police radio." This meant they could listen to what
the police were saying to each other. If there was a robbery,
the police would be talking about it. She turned it on.

As Maggie, Brian, and Tell listened, they heard there was a
robbery last night. It was at a 24-hour convenience store in
Pontotoc. A man with a gun came in and got all the money. It
was 1 AM, right in the middle of the big storm. He ran out of
the store into the darkness, and into a car. A woman was
driving the car. The car drove away fast. The convenience store
worker called the police. Within just two minutes, two police
cars were chasing the robbers' car. It was a close thing. The
police almost caught the robbers. But the night was very dark,

and it was raining hard. The car with the two robbers was going too fast. It went off the road and hit a very large tree. Both the robbers, a man and a woman, were dead.

Tellman Sykes turned white. He put his hands to his face. He could not talk. He sat down. He began to cry. It had to be his dad, and his no-good girlfriend. But no one was sure. The police did not give out names on the radio. Maggie Morningstar called Ranger Jack Madison on the police radio. He answered right away. Maggie asked him, "Where's Tell's little brother? Where's Rio?"

Ranger Madison answered, "We don't know. But he's not in the car. He might be OK. We're looking for him now. The police got a phone call from a motel in Tupelo. Rio may be there."

Willa and Dale came to the ranger's station. They sat down and waited with Tell. No one felt like talking, or going anywhere.

An hour later, Ranger Jack Madison drove up in the park car. Next to him was a little boy. Tell ran out of the ranger's station and pulled the car door open. Inside was Rio. Both boys started crying. By that time, everyone was crying. It was the happiest Brian could remember feeling in a long, long time.

CHAPTER 15

Tellman's and Rio's mother arrived later that day. She was a thin but pretty woman with dark hair. She looked very tired. She was looking for her boys for over three months. But with Dave Sykes moving to a new town every day, it was impossible for the police to find the boys. Now she had her boys back. She was taking them back home to Alabama the next day.

By this time, Darla came to the park to pick up Willa and Dale. They said goodbye to Tell and Rio. Willa wrote down Tell's e-mail address on her hand with a pen. Tell promised to stay in touch. He could not stop hugging Rio. Rio was small for a seven-year-old. He had not been eating well, probably.

That night, Brian drove to Pontotoc to have dinner with Darla. She left Willa and Dale back at the motel. They could watch TV or work on Darla's laptop computer.

Darla told Brian that her husband Rick called last night. She said, "He says he's changed his mind. He really does love me. He wants me to come back to Indiana."

Brian said, "How do you feel about that?"

Darla said, slowly, "I don't know. What if he changes his mind again? And Willa and Dale are starting to get used to Mississippi, and not having their dad around. And, I'm not sure if I can feel the same way about him. He left me once. He could do it again, and hurt me."

"Right," Brian said. "I get that." After a minute, he added, "Why not wait for another week? It'll be July then. If Rick really wants you back, let him come here. He has a truck. He can drive to Mississippi if he really wants to."

Darla smiled. "You're right," she said. "That's what I'll do."

After Brian got home from dinner, Ranger Jack Madison came to visit Lakeside Campground. He said, "Dave Sykes and his girlfriend stayed at a motel in Tupelo. They left Rio at the motel. Then they went to rob the convenience store in Pontotoc."

"Do you think they were going to go back and pick Rio up?" Brian asked.

"I asked the same question," Jack Madison said. "But my friends in the police said their car was going in the wrong direction when they left the store. There were driving away from the motel, off to the south. I think they left Rio at the motel and didn't plan to go back."

Both men were quiet for a minute. Then Brian said, "Just like they left Handy, and then Tell. Just left them."

"Right," Ranger Jack Madison said. "But now Dave Sykes is dead. And it's over. Tell and Rio are back with their mom. Now they can go home."

CHAPTER 16

That night, there were more storms. There was strong wind and rain for a while, and then it got quiet. Then it rained and blew again. There were few campers at Trace State Park tonight. The TV said there would be storms for the next two days. No one wanted to camp out or go fishing during strong storms like that.

In between storms, Brian walked over to the Opa Campground. He walked under the dark trees. The air was washed clean from the storm. There were only a few mosquitoes. It was very cool. He could smell the lake. If he listened hard, he could another storm coming. It was still far away, to the west. "This is a beautiful spot," he thought. "If the park brought electricity and water back here, more campers might want to stay." As he thought this, he heard two owls calling, far, far away, across the lake. Two people died last night. And two owls called. "It's just an old story," he thought, "but what if...?"

He walked back to Lakeside Campground and saw the lights in his trailer. He thought about his wife, Nancy, and how much he missed her. He thought about his friends at Trace State Park, and in Pontotoc, and in Tupelo. Mississippi was nothing like his home up north. He never thought he would live at a state park in Mississippi, of all places. But he loved the lake. And he loved his job. He loved living at Trace.

He thought about Handy the dog, who was leaving with Tell and Rio to go back home. It was time for Brian to get his own dog. He would start looking, tomorrow. Maybe Willa and Dale would help him.

BOOKS IN THIS SERIES

American Chapters books by Greta Gorsuch

The Bee Creek Blues & Meridian
Lights at Chickasaw Point & The Two Garcons
Living at Trace
Summer in Cimarron & Lunch at the Dixie Diner
Cecilia's House
The Storm